SURROUNDED

BY

INSPIRATION

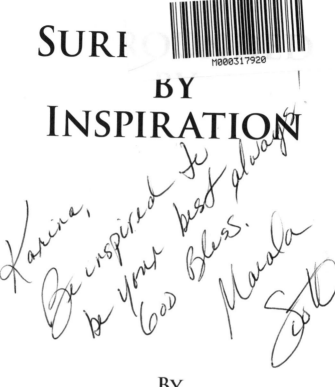

Karina,
Be inspired to
be your best always.
God Bless.
Marala
Scott

BY

MARALA SCOTT

Cover Design by: Neil Noah
Copyediting by: Tracy Riva

Library of Congress Control Number: 2012937459

ISBN 13: 978-0-9820268-2-3 (print)
ISBN 13: 978-0-9820268-5-4 (ePUB)
ISBN 13: 978-0-9820268-6-1 (ePDF)

For information regarding special discounts for bulk purchases of this book for educational or gift purposes, as a charitable donation, or to arrange a speaking event with the author, please contact Jeff@maralascott.com

www.maralascott.com

DEDICATION

To my gorgeous husband, who encouraged me to share my inspirational quotes in hope that others benefit as I have. Every morning when I open my eyes I begin my day with beautiful inspiration, you sweetheart. I treasure the loving words we speak to one another each morning. Thank you for your love and constant faith in me. To have you is to have pure love all the time. Our time together is nothing less than adventurous, loving, fun and filled with inspiration. I love you Tré.

My beautiful and loving children Aaron and Alyssa, you've always been surrounded by God's inspiration. Although you may not have known it, you've been mine. God has touched your lives in many magnificent ways. You must continue to trust God and see His inspiration for what it is, a way to achieve peace, happiness, love, and faith. You've heard these messages throughout the years until you've felt the power of them taking shape in your own lives. Aaron, I started writing these quotes because of you son. You are an amazing writer and need to share your compassionate words of wisdom to inspire others as you have me. Alyssa, you are very humble and keep your brilliance to yourself. It's beautiful and powerful so share it, as I've learned from it. Help others with it as you've helped and inspired me.

For those that seek inspiration this is meant to remind you to take the higher ground so you can look down and see the beauty and gifts planted in and around us from God. Receive that you are surrounded by inspiration. See it, feel it, and smell it in the air. Use it to heal and help you reach your goals of being a stronger, healthier, and much happier person.

SPECIAL ACKNOWLEDGMENT

A special thank you to the beautiful and talented Italia Gandolfo. Your love, faith, guidance, and shared passion is so greatly appreciated. You are a part of the inspiration we are surrounded by.

With an Abundance of Love,
Marala Scott

FOREWORD

Marala Scott is an amazing, successful, and beautiful individual with a very special ability to help others see the truth in their lives and motivate them to take action to improve themselves. Through her memoir, *In Our House, Perception vs. Reality*, she shared some of the most challenging aspects of her life so that she may be able to inspire others who were going through their own struggles. For her work Marala Scott became one of Oprah's Ambassadors of Hope, was awarded WNCI radio – Sunny 95's 20 Outstanding Women You Should Know, and received numerous congressional and literary awards.

Her communication style and advice on life, people, relationships, faith, etc. is truly unique. It's direct, truthful, and raw. Marala would rather be honest and try to help you than tell you what you want to hear. Some people can't handle Marala's insights because they don't listen to God and trust their faith or they don't want to deal with the facts.

As her husband, I have seen her actions impact my life and the lives of so many others. She has been an Angel to me. The lessons I have learned about faith, forgiveness, truth, people, and following your God-given intuition are now part of who I am and want to be. Whether it has been through her writing, speaking, retreats, or inspirationational posts, I have seen Marala Scott change and save lives. There hasn't been a speaking engagement or retreat where Marala hasn't taken individual time with someone she just met in order to help him or her. Within minutes, the individual would be crying, sharing his or her most tragic secrets, in hope that Marala would help them overcome the hurt.

What many people don't know about Marala Scott is how silly and playful she is as an adult. Maybe this is because she wasn't able to be "free" as a child; or maybe she cherishes life and doesn't take for granted the ability to see God's beauty. Often, you can find Marala walking on a beach collecting shells or sand dollars.

The inspirational quotes found in this book came from Marala helping others or revealing what God put on her heart. We want to share many of these messages with you so that you may live a happier life, open your eyes and heart to God, and be *Surrounded by Inspiration*.

Tré Parker

Introduction

In our lifetime one thing that is incontestably guaranteed is the myriad of emotional experiences that we are destined to have. For me, a barrage of them have been agonizing while others have proven to be nothing less than amazing. One thing I know for sure is that regardless of where I've been, or what I have gone through, I've always been surrounded by inspiration.

When I didn't think it possible, inspiration has made me look up instead of down. It's caused me to laugh when I was already crying. It brought back the ability for me to feel when I was numb and I was always able to prevail when I was inspired to grasp that I wasn't the only one.

As time went by I was able to reflect on everything that I thought was difficult, traumatizing and unattainable only to realize that I'd made it through everything I believed I wouldn't. There were times that the darkness was so impenetrable I couldn't help but feel alone, only I wasn't. It wasn't until I learned how to sense the presence of God that I realized I was never alone. I voluntarily entered into the realm of seeing things in a positive way instead of in a manner that complimented whatever disposition I had. Regardless, the end result has always remained the same. I am surrounded by inspiration and I choose to see and use it.

It's not as complicated as you would think to perceive this. I can only tell you how *I* felt the presence of God. It was with the silent brush of merely a single word against my spirit, *faith*. Close your eyes, take a deep breath and exhale. Then open your eyes, look around and observe your surroundings. Take into account everything you see. Your life may be extremely challenging at this time. Your spirit may be blocked by burden, pain, self-pity or anger. Now, close your eyes and try again. But first, think about what you would have if you didn't have, what you have, meaning anything. Take that deep breath all over again and go over to your window and look outside. Let your heart and mind have faith there is something more beautiful and inspirational than what you presently see. Release your mind and everything negative in it. Let your thoughts wander free for a moment and find something beautiful. The painted sky, vibrant trees, chirping birds, luscious grass, and colorful flowers all got here some way. The same way they are here, God is too. He made them and He made you. Think about the neighbor across the way who was unemployed for a long time but kept his positive demeanor and his head held high through all of his mounting adversities. Finally the career he prayed for presented itself. I'm sure you've heard of that beautiful little boy with the deep brown eyes that had a painful bout with cancer for the longest time, but ultimately he beat it. There are countless stories of inspiration to feed your soul. Inspiration is simply another way to look at your life with a positive approach so you can know and appreciate exactly what's in it. Inspiration has a divine influence on the mind and spirit. If something can inspire you, use it to become a better you. Don't just look at it and go away.

I share what I know as I've learned it. The inspiration I select to distribute was born here on this earth in the form of God's creation. It filters freely through my heart as a constant flowing reminder of the truth. It is what has helped shape me into accepting the power of inspiration, using it to live a healthier, and happier life than the way it began. If you don't know, read my memoir, *In Our House: Perception vs. Reality* and you'll better understand how powerful inspiration is for me. You'll appreciate with conviction that the way it's changed my unimaginable life, it will help you too, if you'll allow it.

These words are my lessons and living them converts situations from negative to positive. When you breathe them they'll consume you from one day to the next. I pray you are able to see them for what they are and hear the truth in them. They are open to your own interpretation as well.

In my unfathomable journey through life I've been blessed with the opportunity to meet many. I see things from a very different viewpoint than most, but the gift to see came from God. I've met people that were beyond exhausted with life and I've met others that have celebrated it without giving thought to anyone other than themself. I've met numerous people who care about others, this planet, and everything around them unselfishly. I've met those that don't want to care about much other than surviving. They can't reach for inspiration because they don't believe it belongs in their world. They chose not to have faith and decided to be unhappy.

The one thing they all had in common is that they were searching for something to believe in or hold onto. The only thing I could give them was evidence of my faith and how it has worked in my life. Faith is the beginning of growing your spirit by taking it to a higher level. Instead of looking around for something to believe in, faith gives you the power to believe in yourself and the promise of God. Faith is powerful. And that power can drive you to seeing and experiencing more than most do in a lifetime because your level of expectations are higher and you will live without doubt.

These words of inspiration come from random phases in my life. I have shared them openly with many of you and I've been asked the same question. Why don't you publish a book of all of your quotes? Well for all of you that have asked, here they are. They are meant to breathe and take shape whenever and wherever they land. Should that be in your heart or spirit, then like me, they are meant for you too. Remember that regardless of what you go through in life you are always surrounded by inspiration! Embrace God's gift to you.

With Love,
Marala

FAITH

Faith is a living and breathing mechanism that is necessary to progress. Without it you'll feel a constant emptiness. —Marala Scott

There was a point in my life that I had little to no faith. I was going through the most traumatic time of my life, which is chronicled, in my memoir *In Our House: Perception vs. Reality*. I recalled all of the horrific things my mother was transitioning through and unknowingly she was dragging me through them with her. Before the horror with my mother began she was full of faith in God, but what happened to her challenged my faith in Him, but only for a brief time. It wasn't until I truly had nowhere to turn that I grew angry with God and I told Him so. In the middle of my bluster of words, I felt a calmness explaining what was happening must occur, as it was a part of her fate. God's arms embraced me in a way I'd never experienced and won't ever forget and that was the beginning of me becoming the person I love. Faith in Him is what brought me through all of the tragedy I've had and there has been a lot. The negative experiences I had didn't end as a child but neither did my faith. In times of trouble and in times of joy, seek God by having faith that He is always present and you will make it through. These words came from such moments.

This life is yours. You're the one that should write the script and play the leading role. If you need help with the script, ask God. —Marala Scott

Lift your hands, head, voice, heart, and spirit! Life is worth celebrating. Don't waste time pointing out the pain and dwelling on it. Life is what you make it and you see what you choose to. Make today a day for having a new vision of passion, faith, forgiveness and love. —Marala Scott

God places good people in your life! The bad ones come by your invitation. —Marala Scott

Don't allow your boundaries to become blurred or compromised. Stay true to who you are. That is a test of your character. —Marala Scott

Sometimes we take a hard stance on certain situations but when that very situation occurs in our own life, that is a defining moment. That's when we are tested. Hold on tightly to your faith and commitment to God. Don't forget the boundaries when it's convenient so you can get or do what you want.

Because someone else couldn't, doesn't mean you can't. That's how greatness is achieved. Reach for your goals with all of your passion and you'll find your purpose! —Marala Scott

Don't waste this precious life complaining. Put into today effort that will help make it better tomorrow. Progression changes things. —Marala Scott

So much energy goes into complaining about what you can't change. Sometimes, it's just too big an issue for you but it's never too big for God if you believe. Do something that will walk you around your problems so that tomorrow will be better. Focus on results instead of unnecessary talk or tomorrow you'll be in the same place with the same complaints.

Forgiveness is powerful and hate is too, but one heals and the other destroys. Determine what end you want to be on because they both affect your life and that of others. Lessen the burden on your spirit by carrying less anger and more love instead. Don't hold yourself hostage to what impedes your growth. —Marala Scott

You are stronger and wiser than you've been told. Your passion for God is what you must hold on to because it can remove everything that will keep you from living a beautiful and productive life. Your smile lights up a room when you use it. Your heart loves to laugh. Music opens your soul and allows happiness to dance through it. Remember who you are. You are a giver, helper, and true friend. Determine what you are here for and what it is that you want to leave behind. —Marala Scott

Don't let your fear keep you from your intended success. Fear is a state of mind that you make a choice to have. It can hold you hostage and stop your progress. Desire to live free by choosing to be fearless!
—Marala Scott

I met a young man that had more talent than he ever knew. He could accomplish just about anything he wanted with a reveled passion. Once he did so, his passion would dissipate as quickly as it came. The reason was that he'd always achieve something that no one thought he could. Once he made it into the realm he fought for and realized he had to maintain it, he'd quit before he failed. He kept walking away from his dreams.

Don't wander through life wondering what you're here for. Regardless of who you are, add to history by leaving your own powerful imprint like that on a sand dollar. Read about our history and evolution, understand it and then add to it by sharing your own testimony, strength, courage and wisdom. Leave your name in the books. —Marala Scott

My childhood was horrific and I really couldn't understand why everything happened the way it did. I couldn't fathom that it occurred *In Our House* behind closed doors with none of it being noticed or cared about by anyone. But I did survive and it was meant for me to in order to share my story so that others could be warned of what happens behind closed doors. It took strength to tell my story but more importantly it took faith in God. I left my imprint to help others so that my mother's life would not be in vain. I pray you leave yours as well. There are endless and powerful ways to help others.

Trust and faith in man are hard to come by. You can find yourself disappointed and hurt because of following your heart. Trust and faith in God aren't hard to come by because they're already instilled in you and He knows your heart. Simply, trust God and you won't have errors in your decisions. —Marala Scott

You will always have choices. While some are easy and others may be very difficult, the fact remains that they still have to be made. Take time and reflect before making a decision about something that will affect your life, love, faith and trust towards others. It's your choice so if it doesn't work out don't blame anyone else. Think before you speak, judge, or commit. Have faith in your God given intuition and trust it completely when making choices. —Marala Scott

Material things are nice to have but don't confuse them with happiness. When you put your material things away or are done with them for the moment, they don't go where your peace and happiness lives, inside of you. Take time to make yourself happy and live in a peaceful state. Change your focus from material things to God. —Marala Scott

There is a young lady that writes me quite regularly. Her dilemma is simple, she's married to a man that she doesn't have much, if any affection for; however, she has all of the material things some would want. Her relationship with God has been sitting on the bench for so long she's forgotten which bench. Don't compromise your values or happiness for material things. As you get older, you realize the significance that love, just real pure faithful love, can have.

When you go to sleep tonight take flight into your dreams so when you awaken you can accomplish your goals. —Marala Scott

Don't say love will never happen or you'll never see it. If you're a negative person, move to the state of I Am or I Can instead of living in the state of, I Can't, I Don't or I Won't. Just be open to believing in the best as it's already in front of you. Believe you will receive what you are seeking. —Marala Scott

God connects and disconnects you from other people all the time. Don't try and plug yourself into someone or something He has unplugged you from. Everyone and everything isn't good for you. God can save you from yourself and bad choices if you trust in Him. —Marala Scott

Through random conversations people often share with me things that cause them to hurt. One of the commonalities is when people they've trusted and loved have abandoned them at times they've needed them most. They realize they've been there for those very people, helping them through challenging situations. They were loyal, caring and faithful. But the very moment they blinked their eyes, the person they fought to help disappeared like the summer sun at night when they needed the compassion and help returned. We don't always know when to let go so God will do it for you. Understand that you are meant to be who you are. Give without expecting a return on investment. Someone else may return the love and thoughtfulness to you and it may be a stranger. Be thankful. Don't measure kindness. Recognize and appreciate it.

Life is a beautiful gift from God and how you see it depends upon how you've decided to live it. Don't blame others. Make changes today. Put God first and everything will fall into place like beautiful snowflakes. You're destined to achieve greatness, if you do this. —Marala Scott

We live in a world that shows so little faith. Change it by showing yours. Trusting your God-given intuition is trusting God. Your faith is proven by your actions so believe. —Marala Scott

Don't pray for something you're not ready to receive. When you pray for something and God gives you the solution or what you've asked for, accept it. Not responding to God is the same as ignoring Him. Don't keep making that mistake because you don't like what He shows, tells, or gives you. Have obedience with your faith. —Marala Scott

Obedience displays humility. Love will breed passion. Faith reveals obedience, humility, love and passion for God. —Marala Scott

Fear of failure is a state of mind that settles in you if you permit it. Friends that are disloyal are in your circle because you allowed them. Relationships void of trust, love and respect exist when you accept them. Misery happens when you keep company with it. Anger and hate manifest when you don't receive the power of forgiveness. Darkness occurs when you don't allow God to be the light that you follow. —Marala Scott

When you receive that others can pray for and love you even if you've never met them, you are receiving the gift of God working in your life through others. I am sending you a smile, love, hugs, and prayers for faith, success, peace, good health, and happiness. —Marala Scott

Empower yourself by releasing yourself. Don't let others control your emotions or dictate the path your life is taking. Use and believe in the power of the words I Am to show faith in yourself. Find yourself and love that person. Be present in this amazing journey of life. —Marala Scott

Since everything began in my father's house, a lot of the blame was given to him for not doing what I believed was the right thing. But once I was no longer a child, I was in charge of my life, as my father was his. Every hurtful and demeaning thing he said I was, I retrained myself to believe that I was not. Everything he said I was incapable of accomplishing didn't matter because he couldn't see the strength inside of me. He didn't control the journey that God gave to me although he helped me get to the point where I was desperate to see what I needed, which was inspiration. I was surrounded by it more than I knew. Because I was in pain my focus was negative. Empowering yourself is something you must find the internal strength to do. Once you learn to do that you will stop blaming others for your failures because you will take ownership of your life and focus on success. Draw from the inspiration around you to progress.

Miracles happen in your life daily, yet it's up to you to see and appreciate them. Everyday you wake up is a miracle. Recognize the gifts in your life and draw positive energy from them. Your problems come from focusing on problems. Don't focus on and discuss what you cannot change. We have so much more to be thankful for, and encouraged by, instead of complain about. See it, feel it, and love it. —Marala Scott

I was having a Women's Retreat one weekend in May last year. The day before the women were coming in from all over the country I had a doctor's appointment. I found out that I had multiple brain aneurysms that needed immediate surgery. I wasn't ready for what I heard and became a tad numb. I decided to delay the surgery because I hadn't digested it yet. I told the doctor I'd call him when I was ready for surgery but asked when I should have it done, as they had grown significantly since first discovered. He said he would've already done it and wanted to schedule it immediately. I refused and left the office with a nervous smile. I told my husband I wasn't ready and couldn't do it. After I spoke those words, I felt a hand on my shoulder and a voice in my ear that said, "Do it now." This was God talking to me. When I stopped at a stoplight, I pulled out the surgeon's number and scheduled the surgery immediately. It would be done after the retreat that weekend. On Monday night, I completely shaved my head and confidently put my life in God's hands. Tuesday morning I entered the surgery with barely a handful of people knowing. I went into surgery without a trace of fear, and came out of it filled with God's favor, love, mercy and inspiration. He inspired me a long time ago to have complete faith. You can trust Him if you can hear Him. Listen carefully as He speaks to us always.

This life is a huge canvas for you to create any masterpiece you want and leave your mark in any way you deem. Create with passion, honesty, love and appreciation for what God has allowed you to experience. You cannot change history but you can add to the final outcome by changing your future. Share your gift of life with love. —Marala Scott

Don't stay on the road that isn't paved the way you want. Use the tools you have to pave it again or simply take another route. —Marala Scott

I know of several women, as well as, a few men that are in unhealthy life situations. They don't like it, but won't do anything to change it. Their painful words are sadly consistent. I tell them that there's always an alternate route, even if you have to construct it yourself. Don't be afraid to put in the work for your future. It's your happiness and peace of mind that is in jeopardy.

Fear can paralyze you and keep you exactly where you are. Others use your fear as a stepping-stone for themselves. Don't let this negative state of mind hold you hostage so that you don't progress, heal, laugh, love, and inspire others. Your mind is a powerful tool so use your faith instead of talking about it and move past the fear. —Marala Scott

A very intelligent and faithful man once told me that he wasn't willing to be in a long-term relationship because he'd been cheated on. I told him he didn't know what he could be missing if he didn't take the time to invest in what's known as life, again. I explained that everyone has warning signs to what their personality is like and he simply needed to pay closer attention to them. But once you tell someone what your fear is and why, most often they will use it against you if you allow it. Don't let fear of failure keep you from moving forward. You may find exactly what you never thought you'd have the next time around and it may very well be a gift from God. Don't be afraid of progress. Try not to make the same mistakes.

When you are taking steps of progress you will have moments where you may take a step or two backwards. Don't be discouraged. This is how you're made to be stronger. Challenges that cause you to work harder to overcome them keep you thinking, working and appreciating. Don't ever give up. Look behind you and see what you've already done and keep going. Progress is a constant movement.
—Marala Scott

Forgiveness is the root of happiness and freedom for oneself. —Marala Scott

If you wait for someone to support your goals and dreams you may never reach them. Believe that you have everything it takes already to accomplish anything you want. The fact that you have goals and dreams means you crave something more for yourself. Put your passion into action and make things happen. Achieve it by believing in yourself.
—Marala Scott

If you think your day will be stressful, it will be. Change your thinking and commit to it being a great day and it will be! —Marala Scott

Sometimes I wake up with specific things on my mind. It doesn't take long before I realize that thinking about negative issues is already shaping my day. So I begin again with something that makes me laugh or brings me into focus on something that's positive and progressive. After that, my day is exactly what I want it to be because *I* shaped it. It really is that simple. There are many things I can control, but many more that I can't and those are the things I leave in God's hands and He always works it out.

It's not prudent to try and accomplish goals just to prove something to someone that didn't believe in you in the first place. Whatever you chose to do in life, do it for yourself. Do it because you believe in your own abilities, strength, and passion for success. If you need someone to believe in you and they stop or no longer care, your drive to reach your goals may end. —Marala Scott

When you lay your head down to sleep tonight, place your problems and worries in His hands. With tomorrow's dawn, let each breath you take be your reminder that life alone is your inspiration to do and be the best person you can be. Each day brings a new opportunity. Don't live in the past or be afraid to forgive someone, correct a lie, say you're sorry, make a new friend, tell someone you love them, and go after your dreams. —Marala Scott

How can you expect or desire something of someone that you don't do or have yourself? People want honesty but they aren't honest themselves. They want successful partners and spouses but don't work towards their own success. They want happiness but are not happy. The list goes on and the point is, change your mindset, goals, and drive so you can have it all. It begins with you. —Marala Scott

Make today what you want it to be. Don't accept what it turns out to be. —Marala Scott

Shape your mind, body and day. Happiness begins when you invest in being happy. If you don't shape your day, it'll take shape on its own and you may not be happy with the results.

When you wake up tomorrow you are going to have the most amazing gift. Don't waste it or take it for granted. It's life! Enjoy God's gift. —Marala Scott

Having brain surgery was a reminder of what a gift my life is. I can still do and be anything I choose. It should never take a tragedy to remind you of how precious life is. I've always known, but when something happens, the taste of life is savored so much more. Don't wait on a tragedy to make life taste better. I see and appreciate more than before and didn't realize it until after my time was extended.

It's time for you to do something amazing for yourself. Believe! Keep all of those negative thoughts and energy away from you. Believe that you will have a fabulous life full of eye-opening revelations and you will. Reinvest in your own health and well-being. Love yourself and enjoy all that is healthy for you. —Marala Scott

We all have our personal navigation system to help us stay on the right path and away from anyone or anything that is a negative influence. Stop trying to find your own way around life making unnecessary mistakes that damage you. Follow your God-given intuition. You have to trust it to follow it. We trust our GPS why not GOD. —Marala Scott

People that know me have seen my trust in my God-given intuition first hand. I've had so many experiences where God has spoken to me and I don't hesitate to listen and accept His words of warning. I may not always understand why whatever He is telling or showing me conflicts with what I innately want to do. However, I've learned that it doesn't matter because it's already been proven that intuition rises above reason. I can't explain it, but I trust it. The few times I haven't, I regretted it. My son and daughter have seen the results of trusting it and not trusting it first hand. They know my position and now follow their God-given intuition as their own personal GPS. God speaks to us; it's just up to us to hear him.

Great opportunities spawn from little opportunities. Think bigger than your original idea and go for it! —Marala Scott

Grab success by thinking outside of the scope of things that hold you emotionally hostage. Let your mind work without limits. —Marala Scott

At times you may have to go against the current, which takes faith because you have to keep fighting to survive. It will only make you stronger when you do and that strength will be useful later. —Marala Scott

Nothing or no one is hopeless. When we believe it is or he or she is we have simply given up on ourselves and lost hope. —Marala Scott

Create a fulfilling plan and inspirational journey for your life before your life chooses a plan and journey for you. It may not be one you want. —Marala Scott

RELATIONSHIPS

Relationships will never work without two people being in it for the right reasons. If you don't have true love, faith, and trust you are setting yourself up for failure. —Marala Scott

I was always cautious of people in general, especially after what happened to my mother. The people she allowed in her life, for one reason or another, contributed to the tremendous destruction of it. Watching her demise led me to be cognizant of whom I let in my life in addition to my inner circle. People have the ability to influence you even if you won't acknowledge it. It takes a strong mind and heart to resist negativity such as greed, infidelity, harmful gossip, and lying just to mention a few. Knowing the difference between friends and associates is the beginning of having healthy relationships. Taking time to know the person you are intimate with is vital to your long-term happiness and well-being. Relationships aren't items you throw away when you're done with them because they can come back to hurt you at any time in your life. The safest and best relationship to have is with God. When you have problems that are too personal and difficult to share with man, share them with God. You have to be in the relationship for the right reason or it won't work out. Be honest about your intentions. Don't use people or you'll end up being used. Have faith that you are making good choices in your relationships by paying attention.

No one can take from you what you aren't willing to give. No one can see weakness in you that they can use and manipulate if you don't have it or show it. No one can strip you of your faith if you truly have it to begin with. No one controls you except for you. No one can make you happy if you don't make yourself happy. No one can push you down a path you aren't willing to walk. Take responsibility and control of your life. —Marala Scott

More often than anything else I tell people to stop blaming others. It's human nature for people to take what you offer. If it's sex, it's sex. If it's money, they'll take that too. But don't go behind them and blame people as though you are the victim if you're giving it away. Look at their warning signs and think about what you're telling them by your own behaviors. No one can take from you what you're not willing to give. They cannot take your pride, heart, spirit, faith, mind, or love because God equipped you with those things. Protect those as I've had to. If someone hurts you, but you didn't give them permission to do so, don't let that define you and strip you of your faith or you've given up your control. This works in every aspect of your life. Giving away control helps you remain a victim.

Weak people follow weaker people to use them. Strong people help weak people get stronger. Know who your friends are. —Marala Scott

Find your purpose and live it. The only person that can convince you that you can't do something is you. You are able and capable of accomplishing anything if you believe in yourself and work towards it. Don't break your dream in half. Go all the way through it and begin another. —Marala Scott

This is what I'm doing right now. People have tried to break me the majority of my life but it hasn't happened. It nearly did a couple of times, but God wouldn't let those threats follow through because He knew it wasn't my will. That's why I called on Him. All I want to do is make a difference on an unbelievable level by sharing my life's story. I can't tone down my story to make it palatable; I have to tell it as it was and follow through in faith that you'll understand. I know my purpose and I'm living it. Do the same, it feels right.

People don't really talk about you or think about you as much as you want to believe. So let it go. Looking for stress will cause it. —Marala Scott

Relationships are not something you can really control. It is what it is, unless you both have an unwavering relationship with God before you enter into it. If that wasn't your reality, change it and go to God before the relationship crashes off course. Trying to change someone after you're in the relationship often causes more problems because you told them you accepted who they were when you dove in. Work on yourself and go into a loving relationship led by God. That's where you'll find trust, strength, dedication, faith, and a healthy commitment. Any other way you may find a cheating, abusive, angry, neglectful, manipulative person in your bed. —Marala Scott

Being with a person because you need them or they need you can often lead to having to tolerate other behaviors you dislike. Don't confuse sex with love. The relationship usually isn't constructed on love because it was born out of necessity. If you're in a relationship and you want that person but can take care of yourself and they can do the same, it's most often a healthier love based relationship or friendship. —Marala Scott

People can say they love you all they want, but seek love through actions. Love is a valuable and precious gift but the word is overused throwing very little meaning behind it. Often it's used to camouflage mistakes and deceit to keep a person off-balance and still trusting so they can be manipulated. If someone shows you respect, faith, compassion, affection, and other actions that display love then they love you. Love is powerful but without supporting actions it is nothing. Make sure the actions match the word. Be vigilant of actions because they are truer than words. —Marala Scott

Love doesn't hurt. Love is honest and pure. It encourages, inspires, shares, teaches, and excites. Someone in love with you will not willingly hurt you. They will not demean you or lower your self-esteem. Love is not conditional as it is uncontrollable. True love is beautiful and something that will make you smile through even the most difficult moments. Don't settle for what you try to define as love if it's not. Know your value. —Marala Scott

If you've been in a relationship where your significant other was abusive, cheated, didn't appreciate you, and then left you for someone else or just because, stop hurting. God intervened and removed that person from your life because He knew you wouldn't. Thank Him and be content. Move on and recognize your blessings. All the things you couldn't do with that person, accomplish them now. —Marala Scott

Sometimes we love someone so hard we're willing to overlook their flaws such as infidelity in order to have someone in our life, bed, for financial support or whatever the reason may be. However, you have to know your value and it begins by loving yourself first.

Too many people are afraid of being alone and often settle for relationships and having others around them that aren't necessarily good for them. Being alone is powerful and provides an opportunity for you to see and develop your own strength. Don't be afraid of being alone. It's where you will find your creativity and peace while it allows time for reflection. You'll hear God more clearly. Alone is good. —Marala Scott

Don't talk about people when they're going through difficult times. The time to talk about them is when they've pulled through with strength and courage. Inspire or allow them to share their testimony to God instead of turning it into ugly gossip. No one is without trials and tribulations. Instead of being on the sideline watching someone struggle, offer to help. Share beautiful words of faith instead of ugly words displaying hate. —Marala Scott

Forcing a relationship that's not meant for you to have will ultimately cause hurt. Love doesn't hurt. Learn to be patient. —Marala Scott

You have more to offer than you realize. When you reach down, pull someone up then you'll be surprised at how strong you really are. Using powerful inspirational words is one way to do it. When you reach up, remember God is helping you stand when you find it difficult. Pass along the love and compassion that God continues to show you to others and your life will have more depth and meaning. Acknowledge the beauty and power of what is, instead of the negativity and destruction of what isn't. —Marala Scott

I am who I am because God reached down and pulled me up many times and kept showing me countless inspirational things until I could see them on my own. I have the most miraculous stories to share and so do you, when you decide to see them.

Just because you call someone a friend doesn't mean they're a good one. Don't get upset when you realize someone wasn't what you thought. You knew, but decided to overlook those qualities of gossiping, lying, laziness, complaining, cheating, lack of faith... because they hadn't touched you yet. When someone has negative qualities and you tolerate them as a friend or in your personal relationship sooner or later they'll be used against you. Don't promote negative behavior because you're helping teach someone how to behave. It will come back on you when you least expect it or when you need that person to be a real friend. Keep your circle positive and let it radiate from within. —Marala Scott

Be the kind of friend you want. Demand those beautiful qualities from those that want to be in your life.

If you're in a happy progressive relationship value the person you're with. Love, faith, respect, and trust can be difficult to find so return them with passion. All relationships need a genuine and constant effort to last. If you're single, value the time God has given you to learn and evolve into a stronger more knowledgeable person. It's time you need. Every space isn't meant to have someone in it. Focus on what you haven't accomplished and then make it happen. Bad relationships aren't meant for you to stay and tolerate so know when to go. Strength comes from faith. —Marala Scott

Evaluate your relationships and see what they're doing for you. Determine if they're encouraging, inspiring, loving, positive, progressive, and faith-filled relationships. If so, make sure you are giving the same things back to each of them. Relationships can improve the quality of your life and that of the other person if it's an encouraging one. Of course, things happen and one person may need more of the above than the other at times and that's okay as long as it still has the progressive ingredients. Love is powerful, as it can cause pain, hate, or love. Make sure what you feel and receive is love by knowing what love really is. —Marala Scott

Faith in God with the actions to back it up will help any relationship be its best. If it's not working and there is no sign of effort, make changes. Don't settle for anything less. —Marala Scott

Orchids are rare and beautiful. There are many things you could classify that way but don't. Instead of finding the flaws in people, speak into existence what you love about them. It may be as simple as their hair, shoes, smile, spirit, and humor. Notice positive things instead of something that tears down a person. Remember that God crafted each of us uniquely. When we criticize others we are criticizing His creation. Something as simple as a flower is considered beautiful, but we as people claim to have many imperfections. A flower wakes up beautiful and goes to sleep the same way inside and out. Celebrate your beautiful characteristics and those of someone else from the inside and out. Communicate with inspirational words. —Marala Scott

There are people that you love that may walk out of your life unexpectedly, whether its for someone else, because its no longer working the way they want, they don't love you or for another reason. A friend you need and have always been there for may have excuses or lack of compassion to help see you through when you finally need someone. A family member may focus on someone else because they think you don't need help or won't do what they want. Don't let your spirit be disrupted because when everyone else leaves, God is always there. Understand He's the only one that matters. You may try to walk away from God but He won't leave you because He is in you. —Marala Scott

When someone close to you is angry or going through something that has nothing to do with you, yet you're the target of their negativity, don't engage them or retaliate. Rise above their insecurities, pain, anger or whatever it is and pray with passion for them. If you stay in their pool of problems they'll become yours, like wading in quicksand. Inspire, encourage and love, but rise above it all so it doesn't bring down your self-esteem, positivity, or passion. God can renew and repair anything so talk to Him. Rising above can sometimes mean walking away.
—Marala Scott

Everyone doesn't have the compassionate and caring nature that you have. Sometimes it hurts when others don't return to you what you give freely and sincerely. Understand that's the beauty of who you are and what makes you a loving person. Don't change that or measure them because you have the greatest compassion and love already from God. Focus on Him instead of them. —Marala Scott

There were times I'd wonder why people weren't thoughtful, loving, caring, compassionate, and giving for no reason. Then God showed me that there is a world full of those people but they don't expect anything in return so you don't see them. Sometimes their actions are simply overlooked. That was an eye opener!

If you want to be heard, arguing is not the way. Once you start yelling, walls go up and all you're doing is fighting, and sometimes with yourself. Yelling doesn't get your point across it gets it out louder. Collect your thoughts and emotions before trying to make a point. Peaceful, positive communication is more effective. Don't let anger define you when someone isn't receptive to your message. However, most people are open to an encouraging conversation with inspirational words. —Marala Scott

Everyone has an opinion based on their experiences or what they've witnessed. However, respect the opinions of others, but let your passion for the truth be your guide to an honest spirit and reign. —Marala Scott

When you tell someone what you think about their personal situation don't be judgmental. Listen and learn. Unless someone lived my exact life they would be inclined to pass judgment as to if they believe it or not. That isn't for anyone to judge other than God. The message however, is what's meant to be heard. You may not always agree with it, but you can learn something that perhaps you didn't know. Respect someone's experiences but listen for truth and lessons about life.

Love transcends more than you know. It causes inner peace, a random smile, a beautiful relationship, forgiveness, and an unparalleled relationship with God. If your past relationship didn't work don't turn your back on what you deserve, real love. Don't stay on the same tracks and keep going after the same type of person with similar issues. Love is unique and may be right in front of you. Use your God-given intuition before you open your heart. Don't be closed to returning love. —Marala Scott

There are people that you want to change because you don't like some of their behaviors or who they are. The truth is, you can inspire them and encourage change, but you don't change people. God can, you can't. People can make changes to better themselves but what you can do is make changes to yourself. Changing your negative aspects is a better way to cause others to make changes in the way they view and respond to you. Changing yourself is progression. —Marala Scott

When someone tells you they trust you, let them be able to. Loyalty, privacy, and being able to confide in someone are treasured in a friendship. Give to others what you expect in return, even when you don't get it. Keep loyal, loving, progressive, and honest people around you and you'll have less personal issues. If you have an issue that is so private you can't risk it being shared, confide in God, as you can always trust in Him. Trusting God is never the problem. Having faith is what you want to work on. —Marala Scott

Many people share personal information about someone that they shouldn't. They will tell you what a great friend someone is and in the next sentence communicate a very personal fact that the friend confided in them. When this happens, stop them when they begin sharing something you know is personal or inappropriate. That alone will be a reminder for them to be a more loyal friend. If you want to have friends you have to be a good friend. Politely let them know, I don't think I should be hearing this.

Don't let the worries of today keep you from allowing love to flow out of your mouth and into someone you know or don't. A simple thank you, I love you, I appreciate your kindness, you make me smile, or some gentle words of sincere kindness can change someone's day. Share something beautiful just because you can. It will come right back to you. I'll start ... I love you. —Marala Scott

Stop looking for things not to love about yourself. Concentrate on the things you do best. Love yourself completely before you enter into a relationship or collect friends. People will be less capable of hurting and using you if you have self-love because you will be more protective of yourself and your environment. When you love yourself you truly know how to love someone else for the right reasons. —Marala Scott

If you've loved someone and it didn't work out, don't block your blessings and refuse to truly love again. Use the lessons that came from the relationship and make sure you don't repeat them. Take time to think about what happened. Honest reflection will empower you with the strength and knowledge to protect yourself from unnecessary pain and hurt. Assess character and actions before you dive into a new relationship and talk to God. —Marala Scott

Perception makes all the difference in someone being right or wrong. A person's perception may cause them to see one view as you see another. Open communication can help you arrive at understanding each other's viewpoint, which can be more important than being right or wrong. Take time to listen and request the opportunity to be heard. Don't need to be right just seek to be understood. Shared viewpoints help people learn.   —Marala Scott

As adults we tend to forget that it is easy for us to dismantle a child's viewpoint and make them wrong whether or not they are. The problem with that is you may teach them to become angry, frustrated or shut down from expressing themselves. Adults become angry or argumentative if you don't listen. I've found that people are more likely to learn from you when you learn from them. Being heard and understood is more important than having to be right. Right and wrong is simply a matter of viewpoint. Someone may say the sun is rising while someone else said it just set. You can't argue that.

The words "I'm sorry" and "I forgive you" can cause in-credible reactions, remove layers of pain, and change lives if they are said with sincerity. —Marala Scott

The most insignificant difference to you can mean the world to someone else. Reach out and care about someone. Have a memorable life.   —Marala Scott

Personal Growth

You won't grow unless you can accept that you need to. Continual growth is progress. Progress brings you closer to achieving the necessary. —Marala Scott

There are a lot of things that I want to accomplish, which means I still have many lessons to learn. However, there were times when the only thing that would make me keep moving was looking at my beautiful children. They caused me to triumph over my fears and worries in order to progress forward. I didn't have any excuses when it came to my children. It was my responsibility to take care of them, which meant I had to work. I wanted to give them everything I could so I had to get up and make things happen instead of waiting for them to. Having been a single mother for fifteen of their young years I am extremely proud of them. They understand the power of inspiration and they know how to inspire. Personal growth begins when you believe you can accomplish something and then put in the work to make it happen. I refused to use excuses of what someone didn't do for me because I was always surrounded by inspiration, which motivated me to get it done. I stayed focused on my abilities and what God wanted me to see. Part of my personal growth comes from seeing things as they really are and dealing with them from there. Additionally, it stems from learning self-love and appreciating this gift from God, called life. I can do anything I want and so can you!

People don't define you unless you give them permission to. You don't need anyone to validate you. Do the best you can and look to God for answers, as He alone is your judge. Friends and relationships come and go unless they are bound by faith and true love. Sometimes people have things going on in their own lives that you may not be aware of. Try not to be judgmental. However, God's love never fades into history so don't become upset with the lack of love or compassion others show you because you already have the best in Him, if you trust it. —Marala Scott

Be careful in regards to what you put into your body because it will have a good or bad effect on you while it's there. The same goes for your mind. Protect what you take in. —Marala Scott

If practiced one word can change lives, including yours. Use it with sincerity. Faith, forgiveness, love, honesty, and compassion are just a few. Words have more power than you know. Share them with the true essence of who you are and make a difference. —Marala Scott

There is too much negativity out there and allowing a little to seep into the mix of your life opens the door for a lot more. Keep your door shut and locked on negativity. It won't knock it just comes in if you're willing to listen. Don't partake in it as it's like the plague, it spreads. All it takes is a few little negative words from you and before you know it you will be negative too. —Marala Scott

The best way to have a peaceful and successful day is to begin with peaceful thoughts and prayer. Things that bothered you yesterday need to stay there. A solution may follow today without the emotional attachment of anger and frustration. Give out sincere and soothing words. Show compassion and care about what you do, say, and think. Peace derives from within. Create your environment. Don't play in the toxic one someone else created for you. —Marala Scott

The only distractions you really have in life are those you allow. Manage your life, don't complain about it and remain a victim. —Marala Scott

Face your day with a bit of reality and see things for what they are. It'll help you resolve problems because you won't be making excuses to keep from dealing with them. Accepting reality won't always make you happy, but it will set your burdened spirit free from hidden turmoil. Be honest about life. You can hide it from some people, but not God. The only person you're deceiving is yourself. —Marala Scott

One of the best ways to improve your life is to focus on it instead of complaining about how other people are disrupting it. Complaining doesn't help, so clean your spirit and get ready to take control. You can't control others but you can manage your own life better than you think. Decisions, they belong to you. Who you love, it's your choice, too. Where you live, it's how you think. The friends you have may not be good for you. Everything depends upon your state of mind, effort, and faith with action. Take the lead. Stop being led into a life you aren't choosing to live. —Marala Scott

At some point you'll find it's time for change. The only way for you to enjoy change is to keep moving. Progress comes from evolution. Don't be afraid to change your scenery all the way around, especially with all of the beauty out there. Remember those who have internal beauty share inspiration and love more freely. Don't remain in a state of nothing. Life is a gift measured by time. Don't waste it. —Marala Scott

Make changes in your life or your life will make changes for you that you may not like. The choice is yours so embrace it while you can. Mistakes come from not accepting change. Life is a process that will continue evolving with or without your permission. Change is good if you make it good. —Marala Scott

We all have something powerful, meaningful or heartfelt that inspires or challenges us to be our best. Use that inspiration and share it to open someone's eyes and heart. If you're not willing to push yourself you won't move very far. Grow beyond your comfort zone. There's more to life that God wants us to experience or He wouldn't have created such a vast world of opportunities. —Marala Scott

Years ago I met a young man that had a spirit so burdened that I couldn't see it. He was angry with everyone around him including God. He had lost his mother to cancer, his only brother took his life with a single gunshot over the phone for him to hear, his wife had cheated, and his world was filled with bitterness and anger. At work, he did his job well, but he wouldn't let anyone in. For some reason, I didn't want to be bothered with this young man because he fell outside of my comfort zone, but God pushed him in front of me until I got it. I put my foot in the door to keep it from being slammed shut until I was completely in his lonely world. I worked with this young man in regards to rebuilding his faith and trust in God until finally, he did. His world opened back up and light came in. To this day, I remember the first time I saw him smile, and then laugh. A year later, my spirit became heavy when I was around him or prayed for him, but I didn't know why. Still, I kept him close to me. Through his expressions and words, he was truly very happy with his life. Actually, he often showed up for dinner or to talk, using his open invitation. One day he told me that he reached out to his baby sister. He hadn't spoken with her since his brother's death and he'd told her all about me. She couldn't believe that he finally called her, let alone wanted to see her. She missed him dearly. She made plans to visit him a few weeks later during her college break. I couldn't wait to share in his reunion with the only immediate family he had left. One night I was on my way to sleep but couldn't. I turned on the television and flipped to the news and obediently watched. I didn't know what I was looking for until I saw it. I waited for him and he came pounding on my door shortly after the news aired. When I opened the door he collapsed in my arms, nearly taking me with him. A car accident had killed everyone in the car including his sister on their way to visit him. The car went over a cliff, purely an accident. Although his beautiful sister died, I feared so would he as he'd entertained taking his life many times before we'd met. However, during the time I'd spent with him I explained that he had much to appreciate and value in life. I took his hand and showed him all of the inspiration he was surrounded by and taught him to draw from every bit of it and live a happy life. He acknowledged that all of us will have unpleasant experiences but they won't be the first or the last. That's why it is essential to value what we have while its here and learn as much as we can to strengthen us. Ultimately, he accepted what God was teaching him. He was surrounded by inspiration and had an abundance of reasons to love life and evolve into a stronger, healthier, happier person. God was taking very deep root in him while I was just a mere distraction to open his mind and heart. God's love allowed him to make it through yet another heartfelt tragedy. This time, instead of running from God, he ran even closer to Him. This young man's faith wasn't shaken. Sometimes we don't appreciate what God gives us and has done for us. Many times we don't feel inspired to move past our own pain or self-pity. God works miracles in our lives because He can. If you believe it you will see them more than you've ever imagined. Trust me when I say, we are surrounded by inspiration in the most magnificent ways.

You have to be a true friend to have a true friend. You have to hear people in order to be heard. Be quiet and listen because you'll learn. —Marala Scott

People will find your weaknesses and keep you in that state so they can use you. Don't let your weaknesses be used against you to hinder your progressive journey through life. Weak people keep weaker people around them so they feel empowered. Empower yourself properly by keeping strong, positive, intelligent, healthy, independent people of Christ in your life. Every circle doesn't need to be filled with people. —Marala Scott

What goes in will ultimately come out. Let positivity go in so loving, encouraging words and actions flow out into the universe. Allow negativity to slide in and disparaging, angry, hateful words and actions will stream out with consistency. Words define who you truly are. Be wary of what you take into your mind, body, and heart as it can destroy or heal you and others. —Marala Scott

Life is like a precious stone. It will last forever if you live to seek eternal life with God. Value and use every second of this life and enjoy it. You don't waste your favorite chocolate or candies so don't waste this valuable life on foolishness. Indulge in the sweet taste of life and enjoy it instead of angrily forcing down bitter pieces. —Marala Scott

Don't wait for others to help you accomplish things, get it done yourself. If there is something you want or need but are waiting for someone to do it or give it to you understand that's part of the problem. Be independent as a thinker and use your drive and ability to make things happen. It's easy to complain about what you don't have or want, but stop talking and accomplish the objective. Don't blame any deficiencies in your life on others. It's up to you to make your dreams and goals become a reality. When you look back you'll remember you took flight on your own and landed where you wanted. —Marala Scott

Today is beautiful just like you. Take time to see it. Sometimes we want what we already have or are. That's why reflection is good. —Marala Scott

The night before my brain surgery after I shaved my head, I looked into the mirror and saw my reflection. I desperately wanted what I already had, life. My faith in God is what I saw when I looked deep into my own brown eyes. Reflection is such a powerful thing because many times you will see something different but if you look deep enough you'll see the truth. God's promise is real. He gave me comfort in knowing I would go through that surgery just fine and my reflection displayed the same thing. Your reflection can expose many things you may refuse to see. It displays reality.

People make a conscious decision to hear God and they make a conscious decision not to hear Him when it's convenient. Remember, God is your lifeline so listen closely. —Marala Scott

You can dress up your exterior but God is viewing your interior. If there are things you don't like about others, make sure you don't have those traits yourself. People often deflect undesirable qualities onto others to avoid viewing what they don't like in themselves. Assess whether or not you love yourself the way you are. If not, make changes. Don't talk about it, do it. Even if you love everything about yourself, make changes. We all have room for improvement. Change is good and never-ending. —Marala Scott

There are many things that we can accomplish if we don't waste precious time complaining about them and people. Step over the barriers that are there to keep you from reaching your hand to God and accomplishing your personal goals. Life is meant to be an experience. Don't remain in a situation that makes you unhappy when the opportunity to live with passion and happiness exists for all. Stop complaining about whatever is holding you emotionally hostage and begin rebuilding or progressing. Life is beautiful and so are you. Find your inner peace and dwell in it. Strive to give your best. —Marala Scott

When you're running with people that are unlike your true core sooner or later you'll end up like them. Don't allow negativity to take root in you or the branches that grow will bear unpleasant fruit. Keep company with faith, love, happiness, peace, inspiration and of course, God. Don't let others add burdensome layers of anger, hate, resentment, and doubt on you so that you no longer see or remember who God destined you to be. Love yourself and protect your spirit. —Marala Scott

Think about what you want out of life and then ask yourself why. We came into this life without material things and shall leave it at any time without them. There is more to achieve than collecting material things as there is much more to leave behind, meaning your imprint. God left His beautiful imprint everywhere. Design your own and leave it. —Marala Scott

If you've never seen the beautiful imprint on both sides of a sand dollar I recommend holding one, if only once. What a magnificent imprint with a remarkable history. One of my favorite things to do is search for and collect sand dollars. I love the peaceful sound of the ocean as it lends a perfect environment to talk to God. Find places and spaces that offer solitude so you can connect.

It takes more energy to become angry than it does to be happy. Allow God to fill your heart with peace, love, and strength instead of allowing someone that is unhappy with their life to fill your mind with pessimism. You can't control others but you can manage your own life. Smile today and share some beautiful energy because you have it to share. Send a positive message to someone you know or don't. Love is at your fingertips. —Marala Scott

Oh, if I were able to take one less blood pressure pill for every time I allowed someone or something to unnecessarily upset me, I wouldn't be taking them now! We are in control of our health, mind, and spirituality. Think before you let your blood boil over things you can't control anyways. It took years for me to understand this but by the time I did, it was too late. Don't let things build internally. Serenely breathe before responding and sometimes, a response isn't necessary.

If you feel that you're not accomplishing things that are important to you or moving in the direction that you want, remove the obstacles and get them done. No one is holding you back other than you. When you complain about something that means it's bothering you. Stop complaining and fix it, even if it's your relationship. Don't force things that aren't a natural fit. You don't wear shoes or clothing that doesn't fit. Remember, like clothing, some things are simply seasonal and then they have to go. —Marala Scott

It's easy to point out someone's lack of honesty but check your own levels first. Talking about being honest, telling the truth, and doing what's right means nothing without actions to back it up. Don't hide from the truth or cover it up. Be true to yourself and to others. If you have dishonest people around you, don't blame them when you get caught in their lies because they're your friends. Make respectable choices. —Marala Scott

Don't sermonize something you don't practice. Let others see you walk down the path you recommend even if you have learning curves. Be proud of who you are and use your experiences to progress. Learn to become more compassionate and loving, as well as, stronger, wiser and closer to God. —Marala Scott

Accept that you can learn how to do things right from having done things wrong. Don't be hard on yourself, as it accomplishes nothing if you don't learn from your experiences or choices. Today is simply another day to start fresh and do things right. It's another day to be free. —Marala Scott

Only liars think that telling the truth will hurt people. If the truth is revealed with integrity and consistency it will bring clarity, understanding, and sometimes resolution. Deception is never good and playing with liars will entangle you to do or become the same. Stand in faith that the truth will prevail. It may not make the difference you want it to have, however it keeps your spirit honest and refreshed. —Marala Scott

Taking care of yourself first will allow you to better take care of those you love. When you're unhappy, understand that those around you feel and respond to it. You may think you're giving your children or others the best of you but evaluate your situation because you aren't. Taking time for yourself means loving yourself, achieving your goals, spiritually connecting to God and making yourself happy. Don't rely on others to do it for you. Positive change is liberating and people around you can see and feel that change. —Marala Scott

You want something until you get it and realize what you already had was better. You no longer desire what you were craving once you get it. Don't react with emotions especially when you're upset. Think about or analyze the situation before making decisions that will affect you later. Trading one person in for another before having time to breathe and analyze your decision isn't wise. —Marala Scott

One of the greatest secrets to life is learning to let go. After the pain in your past has occurred, its history. Rebound and set your sight on living with drive and passion. —Marala Scott

It's easy to place blame on others when we don't accomplish things. Take responsibility for your choices and don't rely on excuses to bail you out. Start by being true to who you are. Don't let anyone or anything become the excuse for stopping or blocking your goals. You are stronger than you know. Prove it to yourself and then enjoy the substantial benefits. —Marala Scott

If you close yourself off to experiencing new things you're really missing out on what life has to offer. Simply having an open mind will cause enjoyment. Too often, you may focus on problems because you don't have enough healthy activities to keep your mind in a healthy place. Remove yourself from a stressful environment and live in one that reminds you there is more to you than dealing with problems. Be happier because you truly have many reasons to be. Make the decision to have an adventurous life. You're surrounded by inspiration. Indulge. —Marala Scott

Begin your day by committing yourself to a completely positive state of mind. Regardless of what adversity faces or surprises you, move through or around it. Don't play emotional games with anyone, it's not worth your time or energy. Today, you will rise above and focus on what's important to you. Don't engage in negative battles. Smile and share the positive and powerful side of you. Live, love, and laugh from your core while the world watches you. —Marala Scott

Negative thoughts, emotions and behavior will affect your health. What you don't see can hurt you so be aware of what you're doing to your body by worrying. Don't fret about what you can't change. Invest in changing the things you can, that's when you'll stop stressing about them. What you're doing now affects your health later. This life is precious. Enjoy it in good health. —Marala Scott

You want things to be different, but if they were to change you may not notice because you have too much clutter in your life to see it. Often the things you've prayed for are right inside your personal realm. You need to remove things that are undesirable distractions so you can make room for what you've asked for. Clean your life and you'll be surprised at what you find. It may make you smile! —Marala Scott

Everything that comes out of your mouth will affect others and reflect you. What you put out is what helps to shape this world in either a positive or negative manner. When you don't like something you hear or see, think of your contributions and what you've spewed out. If you want to make a difference, love what flows out your mouth, and you'll love who you are. Don't let hate bait you into being hateful, it takes more effort. —Marala Scott

Be true to yourself by being the real you and showing it to people. Love yourself enough to protect yourself from being used by understanding everyone you love doesn't love you back. Don't expect that you will and can make someone love you. Seek comfort in knowing you already have the greatest love from God, which is more than enough. Celebrate being who you are by loving and protecting yourself. —Marala Scott

If you want peace and happiness open your door and invite them into your life. Stop inviting hate and anger to disrupt your life and then wonder why you're unhappy. It's your choice. You have more power over your situations than you think. Consider what your role is in allowing stress and unhappiness to consume you so you can change it. You deserve to be happy but you can't keep blaming others for your unhappiness. —Marala Scott

Sometimes what we need is right in front of us. We're surrounded by inspiration. Take a look. Own to-day! —Marala Scott

Sometimes we find that people are not what we thought they were. We discover that choices we've made were not good ones. That's the beauty of our life. We make each choice even when we don't think we did. We often see only what we want to see, at that moment. Our choices can affect us for a long time if not a lifetime. Consider the consequences before you make a decision to alter your life. —Marala Scott

It took a long time until I realized that the choices I made affected my children too. I learned that from reflecting on my childhood. You won't always grasp it until it's too late. Think before you react because sometimes there are others in your line of fire that you may not have noticed or considered. I am blessed that I am able to see the results of my choices.

Take a moment and share some inspiration. It won't cost you anything and it can make someone's day even more special than you know. Give someone, even a stranger, the gift of a smile. Hopefully, they will do the same because inspiration is contagious. —Marala Scott

When you are true to yourself, the truth will easily come out in your communications and actions. Being forthright can alleviate unnecessary issues. Start by saying what you genuinely mean to say. It's refreshing to your soul every single time although it may disrupt someone else's. However, you can't lie to spare someone from the truth and in return become a liar because you did. Be honest. —Marala Scott

Honesty is a deep breath of fresh air. The truth may not prevail when you want it to, but it will show itself when it needs to. —Marala Scott

Pay attention to your own actions instead of focusing on the actions of others; you can learn something about yourself that perhaps you didn't see. Sometimes you focus too much on things you can't control. However, you can change or adjust your behaviors so you don't keep making the same mistakes. It will help you with personal growth. —Marala Scott

People talk about negative energy all the time, but do you know that when you smile you change the energy around you to positive. Try it and take time to observe the difference. You'll love it! Just ... smile.
—Marala Scott

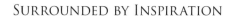

Desperation can make us do wonderful things or terrible things. If you feel desperate seek comfort in God before you make a mistake. —Marala Scott

When you're honest, you don't have to worry about remembering what you said. Keep the words that come out of your mouth truthful. —Marala Scott

When you're broken and weak it's easy for someone or something unhealthy to infiltrate your life. Be strong, have faith in God. When you're on track to achieve your personal goals don't let anything or anyone derail you! Align yourself with success. —Marala Scott

When you make a sacrifice willingly, it means so much more than if you're forced to make a sacrifice that your heart wasn't open to. It reveals something significant about your true character. —Marala Scott

Life is the ultimate test of who we really are and then we're judged for it. Don't view man as your judge. There is truly only one, God. —Marala Scott

We refuse to accept the very things that can help us the most. Learn to be more receptive to wisdom, patience, and truth. —Marala Scott

You can't deceive people for long so don't try to deceive them at all. Simply be the real you. If you don't like who you are, make changes for the better.
—Marala Scott

You'll be surprised what you learn when you listen although it may not be the lesson you want to hear. Trust that it will help you at some point if you remain open to improvement. —Marala Scott

Find the most peaceful place you know and that's where you'll find your spirituality. At times, life can get too noisy and busy to remember where you left it. —Marala Scott

Lose a friend because you told them the truth instead of lying in order to keep one. Real friends speak the truth. —Marala Scott

If you want nothing for yourself but problems and stress so will your associates. Crave success and your true friends will crave it for you and join you on your incredible journey to obtain it. —Marala Scott

Imagine how much positive energy is released when you no longer hold forgiveness captive. People want to know how you do it. Strengthen your relationship with God and He will strengthen you! That's how. —Marala Scott

People think that forgiving someone is letting them off the hook from whatever they did. Contrary, it releases you from being in pain. Trust me I know. I've never felt more liberated! There are things that you will want to be forgiven for, by God. Don't be so quick to oppose this action.

Compromise your morals by trying to convince people your lie is the truth and you'll spend your life convincing yourself to believe your own lies.
—Marala Scott

Peace isn't found outside, it's found within. You can't find peace outside, if you don't have peace within. That's where it originates, God. —Marala Scott

Remember not to take things for granted such as time. Time is not yours as it belongs to God. We often say, I'll do it tomorrow, but remember tomorrow is gifted, not given. Appreciate what time He gifts you with by using it wisely. You never know if you'll need to ask for more. —Marala Scott

FORGIVE

During my journey through life there are many things I've learned but one of the most significant lessons is how and why to forgive. Because of my childhood I had a lot of pain and with pain came the responsibility of carrying a heavy suitcase filled with mistrust, doubt, and anger.

Overall, I didn't really have much faith in people but I could always count on the contents of my luggage. I believed that it would protect me and I relied on them to bail me out of every situation. See, here's how it worked. If I met someone with a wonderful character who presented himself like he was a great candidate to be in a relationship with, I'd simply pull out mistrust. If I needed someone to count on, doubt was always there. But my big protector was anger. Anger was a little greedy as it took up most of the suitcase. It kept me from progressing because I had too much of it that I was dragging around. Everywhere I went I just had to take that burdensome piece of luggage with me. Regardless of where I was in life, it didn't take long for me to remember to open my luggage and let the contents run rampant.

One day, I turned around and realized I was alone and tired. I had no one to carry my heavy luggage. No one wanted the burden. Besides, many people had their own luggage. So, I had to keep dragging it along throughout my life allowing the contents to keep holding me back because although I took it everywhere, it wasn't wanted anywhere. With tearful eyes, I dropped to my knees in faith and prayed for God to help me with this problem because I clearly didn't know what to do.

There was one little word that flooded my heart and invaded my heavy spirit. That word was, *forgive*. I grumbled and refused. Why should I? That would be cowardly of me to let the people that hurt me the most off the hook. I can't do that. I won't do that. I'd been carrying the luggage so long that I didn't need anyone to help me. Sure, it would be nice, but forget it. I picked up the tattered handle and dragged my luggage around a little longer until it completely wore me down. My heart was heavy and I was unhappy. I wasn't progressing at the pace I could have been if I didn't have the heavy luggage. I prayed again in faith that God would answer and asked Him to release my spirit from all this pain. He did, but the same little word came yet again, *forgive*.

I was deeply troubled because I thought if I did forgive, it meant everything I'd been through was for nothing. Everyone that hurt me and caused me great pain got off the hook. Just like that, they'd be forgiven for everything they did to me. What about my pain? Surely, I wasn't going to let anyone off the hook. So, you guessed it, a few more long and agonizing years passed with me dragging my luggage. I was a bit unhappier because of mistrust, doubt, and anger. See, they were evolving but I wasn't. The contents sure caused a lot of problems and even some losses. There came a point when I wasn't confident it was worth keeping that luggage anymore so I prayed, again. I knew I'd been asking God for something I wasn't ready to accept until now. This time I opened my heart and asked God to help me because it was too big a task for me to take on alone. He did, as He had before, but it was a process I was finally willing to undertake. I had nothing to lose but mistrust, doubt, and a lot of anger.

I opened the door and let forgiveness seep deep into my heart. I didn't forget anything that happened to me as a child but I realized how many years I wasted dragging the luggage. Everything that was in the past was done. I don't have the power to change history and hanging onto it was unhealthy. My future was now my focus. The forgiving wasn't for anyone other than myself. They'd probably forgotten what they did to me or perhaps they had asked God to be forgiven at some point. Some of the people who hurt me I never even saw again but I thought the burden of carrying that luggage was protecting me. It wasn't. It was destroying me. Just me. I had wasted years, for nothing. Why was I so determined to be angry when I had a wonderful life ahead of me to enjoy. The past was further behind me with each waking day. Forgiving someone is setting yourself free because you really don't understand how much refusing to forgive someone is disrupting your life and your spirit. I knew I'd want God to forgive me and I couldn't continue to be a hypocrite and be unforgiving of others. That didn't make sense.

It wasn't until I let the word *forgive* have true significance in my life that I began to flourish into the person I am today. I was able to let go of that luggage and take any flight I wanted without penalty of a heavy bag. The power mistrust, doubt, and anger have are destructive. The act of forgiving someone is an amazing release to your spirit. When I did, I understood the pain in my past allowed me to help others in my future. Forgive. Try it soon. Don't waste your valuable life the way I did.

Love & Blessings,
Marala Scott